A Discovery Biography

Samuel F. B. Morse
—◆—

Artist-Inventor

by Jean Lee Latham

illustrated by Jo Polseno

CHELSEA JUNIORS
A division of Chelsea House Publishers
New York ◆ Philadelphia

The Discovery Biographies have been prepared under the educational supervision of Mary C. Austin, Ed.D., reading specialist and professor of education, Case Western Reserve University.

Cover illustration: Maria Ruotolo

First Chelsea House edition 1991

1 3 5 7 9 8 6 4 2

ISBN   0-7910-1447-9

Contents

Samuel F. B. Morse: Artist-Inventor

Chapter 1

In Trouble

The bell rang. Classes were over for the day. Finley was going out the door, when the teacher said, "Samuel Finley Breese Morse!"

Finley knew he was in trouble again. It always meant trouble when a teacher used his full name.

How many times had he heard it? He had gone to school since he was four. Now he was eight. At least once a week all those years, he had heard his full name.

He turned to his teacher. "Yes, sir?"

"The principal wants to see you in his office. At once!"

"Yes, sir." Finley marched toward the office. He could feel his heart keeping time to his feet. *Thump! Thump! Thump!*

Why was he always in trouble? He always meant to do better. He knew he ought to "be a credit" to his father. That was not easy. Father was a minister. He was a writer, too. He had written geography books. It was hard to "be a credit" to a minister *and* a writer!

There were other ways he was supposed to "be a credit." Many times Father said, "Remember, Finley, you are from Charlestown, Massachusetts. Be a credit to your city and your state!"

"I *will* do better!" Finley whispered, "I *will* be a credit!" He went into the office.

The principal held out a piece of paper. "Did you make this drawing of me, Finley?"

"You can tell it's a picture of you?" Finley forgot about being scared. "Then I'm drawing better all the time!"

"I can tell it is supposed to be a picture of me, because you put my name on it. Finley, why did your father send you to Andover?"

"To get ready for Phillips Academy, sir."

"And is this the way to get ready? Wasting your time drawing? Do you know how much this school costs your father? Is this the way to pay him for all he is doing for you?"

Finley could not think of any answers. He only knew that he liked to draw. He said, "I'm sorry, sir."

"And you'll promise to do better?"

"Oh, yes, sir!"

"You promised to do better all last year, too, didn't you?"

Finley could not think of an answer to that, either. He said again, "I'm sorry, sir."

"Do you know what day it is tomorrow, Finley?"

That was a question he could answer! Tomorrow would be April 19, 1800. Just twenty-five years ago the American Revolution started. It began with the battle of Lexington. "Yes, sir! I know about the battle of Lexington!"

"Very well. Sit here and write the story of that battle." The principal left Finley alone in the office.

Finley found paper and ink and a quill pen. He found a shaker of sand to dry his ink. He began to write:

"Twenty-five years ago we fought the battle of Lexington. Our farmers hid behind stone walls."

He stopped writing. He turned over the paper. He drew the farmers kneeling behind the stone wall with guns.

"When I am big," he thought, "I'll paint a picture of the battle of Lexington! I'll—"

"Samuel Finley Breese Morse!" It was the principal.

Finley was in trouble again.

Chapter 2

More Trouble

The bell rang. Classes were over for the day at Phillips Academy. Finley started out the door. The teacher said, "Samuel Finley Breese Morse! You are wanted in the office!"

"Just like it was at Andover!" Finley thought. He had promised Father he would do better. He had promised to "set an example" for his younger brother, Sidney.

What was wrong now? He went into the office.

The principal held out a picture of a turtle and a rabbit. "Did you draw this?"

"Yes, sir. It's a picture of me and Sidney, sir."

"What!"

"You remember the story of the tortoise and the hare? Father said once that we are like that. Sidney is the tortoise, and I am the hare."

"Do you remember how the story ended?"

"Yes, sir. The hare lay down and went to sleep. The tortoise won the race."

"That is about what you did at Andover, isn't it?" the principal asked quietly. "How old are you?"

"Eleven, sir."

"And your eight-year-old brother, Sidney, has caught up with you?"

14

"Yes, sir."

"There is no excuse for your grades, Finley. You are one of the brightest boys here. Sometimes you are at the head of your class. Then, a few weeks later, you are at the bottom!"

Finley listened while the principal talked of Father. He listened while the principal praised Sidney. He promised again to do better.

"It will be different when I go to college," he told himself. "At Yale, I *will* do better!"

Chapter 3

Father Says "No!"

Finley sat in a class at Yale College. He tried to keep his mind on the lesson. The professor was talking about electricity. Finley thought about the letter he had written to Father.

"I am nineteen and almost through college. I know I can be a great artist! But there is no place in America to study art. I must have a chancc to see great paintings. Almost all our artists have studied at the Royal Academy in London. Please, may I go to London?"

What if Father would not say "yes"?

"I wish I had done better here in Yale," Finley thought. "But it has been like Phillips Academy, only worse!"

Both his younger brothers, Sidney and Richard, were in Yale, too. He knew he should "set an example" for them. He knew he had not.

"I'll work hard these last two months," he told himself. "Then maybe Father—"

"Mr. Morse!" the professor said. "We are waiting for your answer!"

Finley jumped. "I'm sorry, sir. I did not hear the question."

The professor asked another student. Finley could feel his ears getting red.

After class, he spoke to his teacher. "I'm sorry, sir."

"Do my lectures bore you, Mr. Morse?"

"No, sir! I enjoy them! And I enjoy all the experiments we do with electricity. Sometimes, though, I wonder why we bother with it. What good is electricity?"

"Somebody asked Benjamin Franklin that same question," the professor said. "He answered, '*Sir, what good is a new-born babe?*' "

Finley smiled. "Did he think electricity would grow up some day and amount to something?"

"Mr. Morse, some day electricity will be a giant! It will change the world! Remember that!"

"Yes, sir," Finley promised.

He went to his room. Sidney was there, reading a letter from their father.

"Do I get to go to London?" Finley asked.

Sidney shook his head. "No. You are to work in a bookstore in Boston. I'm sorry, Brother Hare."

Finley smiled. "Thank you, Brother Tortoise. Maybe Washington Allston will talk to Father. Mr. Allston is a fine artist. He says I show real talent."

"I hope you do get to go," Sidney said.

"I've got to!" Finley said. *"I've got to!"*

Chapter 4

Three Thousand Miles

"Dr. Morse," Mr. Allston said, "Finley has real talent. He could be a fine painter. But he needs to study in a good art school. I'd like to take him to London with me, when I go back. He deserves a few years at the Royal Academy."

Father shook his head. "This is no time for Americans to be in London!"

Finley knew there was danger of war. The English were fighting France. They were keeping other countries from trading with France.

English sea captains were stopping American ships. If they found goods for France, they took them. Sometimes they took American sailors, too, and made them work on English ships.

"I know," Mr. Allston said. "If the English don't stop searching our ships, it could mean war. But England does not bother American artists. Benjamin West, president of the Royal Academy, is an American!"

After many talks, Father at last said, "All right, Finley. I shall pay your way for three years of study in London. After that—"

"Don't worry!" Finley said. "Before long, I'll be getting commissions! I mean that people will be *paying* me to paint their portraits!"

Father smiled briefly. "I know about commissions, Finley. But how many American artists can live on their commissions?"

In August of 1811, Finley sat in a big, bare room in London. He started a letter to his family. How long it would be before they got it! It had taken the ship twenty-two days to sail from America to England. It might take a month for a ship to carry his letter back to America. He wrote:

"I wish you could have this letter now. *But three thousand miles are not passed over in an instant.*"

Mr. Allston came by, to take him to meet Mr. West.

"By tomorrow," Finley thought, "I'll be in the Royal Academy!" He found it was not quite that easy.

"First," Mr. West said, "you must do a drawing for our judges. If they like your work, you may enter the school." He gave Finley a small statue. "Suppose you do a drawing of this in black and white chalk."

"I want to do great historical pictures," Finley said.

"The judges want to see a drawing," Mr. West told him. "If you wish, bring your drawing to me first. Then send it to the judges."

Finley thanked him and took the statue home. "It won't be hard to make the drawing," he thought. "I'll be in the school by next week!"

A few days later he took his drawing to Mr. West.

"Very good, sir!" Mr. West said. "Go ahead and finish it."

Finish it! Finley went back to his room. He studied the statue. He studied his drawing. Maybe he *could* do better. There was more to that statue than he had thought!

"I'd better hurry," he muttered. "September will be half over before I get in the school."

November was half over before Mr. West said, "Good! You may send that drawing to the judges. Now, sir, you know what it is to *work*!"

"Yes, sir!" Finley said. "And I'm *going* to work!"

For months he worked early and late. He did stop work one day to celebrate. That was the day England said her captains would stop searching American ships. Now there would be no war!

A month later, sad news came. America had declared war on England. She had started fighting before she knew that England had stopped searching her ships.

Finley thought of his first letter home. *Three thousand miles are not passed over in an instant.* Men were fighting and dying, because news could not travel faster.

He sat with his head in his hands. He sighed, and went back to work. He could not make news travel faster. But he could be a great artist, if he worked hard enough!

Chapter 5

The Statue

After a few months, Finley decided to do a big picture. He would paint the Dying Hercules. He would make his painting six-by-eight feet.

"Model the figure of Hercules in clay, before you start your painting," Mr. Allston told him. "You will find it helps."

"I'm no sculptor!" Finley said. But he modeled the figure.

"Excellent!" Mr. Allston said. "Have some copies made in plaster."

Finley had the copies made. He took one to Mr. West.

"Excellent!" Mr. West said, too. "Send your statue to the show at the Adelphi Gallery!"

Finley thanked him. He sent the statue to the gallery. Then he began work on his painting.

Mr. Allston came by one day. "Let's go see the show at the Adelphi. The Duke of Norfork will be there today to give the prizes. You would like to see the Duke, wouldn't you?"

"I'd rather work on my painting," Finley thought.

But he went to the show. He listened as the Duke named the winners. He clapped for each one.

Then the Duke said, "The first prize goes to a young American. Mr. Samuel Finley Breese Morse has won the gold medal for his statue of the Dying Hercules!"

Dazed, Finley went forward. They were clapping for him! The Duke was pinning the gold medal on his chest!

Finley wrote to his father that night. "You will not have to send me money much longer. I'll be getting commissions!"

But after three years, he still was not earning anything. His father sent him money to stay one more year. But that was *all* he could do, he said.

Finley worked harder than ever. Sometimes he forgot to eat. Sometimes he painted with a brush in one hand and a cup of tea in the other.

He did stop work one day in December of 1814. He celebrated! The war was over! England and America had signed a peace treaty in Belgium!

"Thank heaven the war is over!" he thought. "If news could travel faster, it never would have started!"

Weeks later, sad news reached England. A battle had been fought two weeks after the war ended. It had been fought in New Orleans. People 3,000 miles away had not known the war was over. More than 2,000 men had died, just because news could not travel faster.

Again Finley sat with his head in his hands. Again he went back to his work. He must make good! He must get commissions!

Chapter *6*

"No More Good-By's"

After four years, Finley had to go home. His paintings had been praised. But he was not earning any money in England.

"What now, Finley?" Father asked.

"I'll work here a year," Finley said. "I'll earn enough money to go back."

Someone knocked. Finley went to the door. A man stood there with a pack on his back. He looked tired. He must have walked far. He had been caught in the rain. Mud spotted his trousers.

"Please, sir," he said, "would you like me to paint your portrait? Only fifteen dollars! I have everything right here in my pack!"

Finley laughed, then said, "I'm sorry. I'm an artist, too. You're tired. Come have a cup of tea."

"No, thank you. I must get work to do."

Finley went back to Father's study. "It was a tramp painter. Poor fellow! He has to knock on doors and beg for work! Thank heaven, I won't have to live that way! People will knock on *my* door. I'll open a studio in Boston."

"Do you have enough money left to open a studio?" Father asked.

"I'll have to borrow money for the first month's rent," Finley said. "But that will be all the help I'll need!"

Week after week, he waited in his studio. Month after month, Father paid the rent. At last Finley gave up. Pack on his back, he became a tramp painter, too.

Even then, he knew Father was helping him. In every town, Father's friends would ask him to spend the night. He always had supper and a place to sleep.

Sometimes he had trouble sleeping. He lay awake and worried. How long would he have to paint portraits for fifteen dollars? When could he go back to England? When could he do great historical pictures?

In Concord, New Hampshire, a man said, "You might get a chance to paint Lucrece Walker. She is the prettiest girl in town. She is the best-loved girl, too. Maybe you should not meet her! You might lose your heart!"

Finley smiled. "I'll not think of getting married for a long time!"

Then he met Lucrece! Before he left Concord, they were engaged. Lucrece promised to wait for him. She said she would not get impatient.

But, after a year, Finley *was* impatient. "I'll never earn enough in New England to get married," he told Lucrece. "I'm going to Charleston, South Carolina. I have an uncle there. He says I can get commissions."

Finley went. In the spring, he wrote happily to Lucrece. "Uncle was right! I have earned three thousand dollars! Our troubles are over!"

Late that summer, Finley and Lucrece were married. Finley said again, "Our troubles are over!"

Five years later, he thought of those words. Hard times had struck the country. Nobody wanted to "waste money" on paintings. Finley had a wife and two children to take care of. Little Susan was four. Charles was a baby.

What could he do? How could he take care of his family? His brothers, Sidney and Richard, could not help him. They had just started a newspaper, the New York *Observer*. It was costing a lot of money to get started.

Once more, Finley had to ask Father for help. "I want to go to New York City," he told him. "I think I can earn money there. May Lucrece and the children stay with you? It won't be for long! I'll make a home for them soon!"

Two years passed before he could write:

"Success has come! Soon we'll have a home! We'll be together! There'll be no no more good-by's! You know General Lafayette is visiting America. The people of New York have asked me to paint his portrait. I leave for Washington tomorrow."

In Washington, he heard from Mother: "You have a new son. Lucrece wants him named Finley!"

The next letter came from Father. Lucrece had died very suddenly.

Chapter *7*

On the Good Ship *Sully*

Finley tried to forget his sorrow in work. Often he painted till midnight. Sometimes he walked the streets until dawn. What good was success without Lucrece? What good was a house without her? He tried having little Susan in New York City with him. She cried to go back to her grandmother.

Finley tried to help young artists, too. "Find a place where you can meet and have classes together," he told them. "I'll help you all I can."

At first, a few artists met. Soon, there were three times as many. They named their group the "National Academy of Design." They elected Finley their president.

"You have helped young artists more than anybody else!" they said.

"Helping them has helped me," Finley thought. Sometimes, though, he still could not sleep.

After four years, Finley heard exciting news from Washington. They were building a beautiful Capitol Building. Some day, they would want great historical paintings for it. That was just the kind of painting he had always wanted to do! Now was the time to go back to Europe. He would study and work. Then he would be ready to do a great painting for the Capitol!

Three years later, in 1832, Finley sailed home from Europe on the *Sully*. On shipboard, the passengers sat around and talked. Finley did not listen very often. He was thinking about the painting he would do!

One night, a young Dr. Jackson talked about a Frenchman named Ampère. "He is doing amazing things with a magnet!"

"What's amazing about a magnet?" one man asked. "It's just a piece of iron that does two things. It points to the North Pole. It picks up another piece of iron."

"Ampère makes a magnet with electricity," Dr. Jackson said. "So he calls it an electro-magnet."

"That's nothing new," Finley thought. "I heard Professor Dana talk about an electro-magnet, six years ago, in New York."

"Ampère wraps an iron bar with wire," Dr. Jackson went on. "When he sends electricity through the wire, the iron turns into a magnet. The more wire, the stronger the magnet is. Sometimes he uses miles of very fine wire!"

Somone laughed. "Not *miles* of wire! It would take hours for electricity to go through *miles* of wire!"

"You're wrong!" Dr. Jackson said. *"Electricity goes instantly through any known length of wire!* Just like that!" He snapped his fingers.

Instantly! Finley went out on the deck alone. *Instantly! Through any known length of wire!* That was the answer to sending messages quickly!

"I'll do it!" he said. "I'll find a way to make a telegraph with an electro-magnet!"

He spent every day working on his idea. He wrote down his plan.

1. I can make electricity with a battery.

2. I can send electricity through a wire.

3. No matter how long the wire is, electricity will go through it instantly.

4. I can make an electro-magnet with an iron bar wrapped in wire.

5. When I start the electricity, the bar will pick up iron. When I stop the electricity, the bar will drop the iron.

6. I could stand a mile away and work that electro-magnet instantly! I could make it pick-up-and-drop the iron!

7. I must figure out a way to send messages with the pick-up-and-drop of an electro-magnet!

When the *Sully* reached New York, Finley shook hands with the captain.

"Good-by, sir! Some day soon you'll hear of the electro-magnetic telegraph! Just remember, sir! It was invented on the good ship *Sully*!"

Chapter *8*

Attic Room

Finley left the *Sully* and hurried to his brothers' newspaper office. He told them about the telegraph.

"It sounds like a long, hard job," Sidney said. "How will you live while you work it out?"

"I'll do one painting for the Capitol!" Finley said. "Then I'll have enough money to live on for years."

"The Capitol isn't ready for paintings," Richard told him. "It may be years before it is done."

"Oh . . . " Finley felt as though he had stepped off a cliff in the dark.

"There is a room in the attic of this building," Sidney said. "You could live there for a while."

"Good! I'll live there for two or three months!" Finley said.

After three years, he still lived in the room. One morning, Sidney came up. Finley was at his work bench. He was wrapping cotton thread around a piece of copper wire.

"I wish I could buy wire already made," he said. "It takes forever to insulate it! I have to wrap it in cotton, so the electricity can't escape."

"Hold out your hands, Brother Hare."

Finley did. His fingers shook. "I'm just a little tired," he said.

"You can't paint with shaky hands," Sidney said. "You need to paint to earn money. When you *do* have money, you can pay men to help you work on the telegraph. Stop working on it for a while."

"I can't stop! I can't think of anything else!"

Sidney held out a letter. "This came for you."

The letter was from the new University of the City of New York. They wanted Finley to teach there. They could not pay him at first. His salary would come from giving private lessons to art students.

Finley went to the university. But he took along his wires and batteries. He still worked on his telegraph.

He did not have many students. He was so poor that he cooked his food in his room.

He always waited till after dark to go for food. He did not want people to know how poor he was.

By 1836, he had a kind of telegraph. He had been working on it for four years! He had two machines, connected with wire. The first machine started and stopped electricity. The electricity went through the wire. Then the second machine pulled a strip of paper tape along, under a pencil. The pencil would go up and down, as the electricity started and stopped. The pencil made marks on the paper tape.

One night, Finley showed his telegraph to Mr. Gale, another professor at the university.

"It's a wonderful idea!" Mr. Gale said. "Could you use some help? I don't have much money. But I *do* have some ideas!"

"We'll be partners!" Finley's voice shook.
It was the first time anybody had offered to
help.

Chapter 9

"Interesting Stunt!"

Mr. Gale *did* "have some ideas." Soon the telegraph was working better. "What we need now," he said, "is a partner with money."

Finley got a letter from Washington. "Gale!" he shouted. "We'll have our money! They are choosing the artists to do the Capitol paintings! Soon I'll have a commission and ten thousand dollars!"

Two weeks later Finley's friend wrote again from Washington. "There was a lot of hard feeling about the Capitol paintings.

One man thought we ought to ask foreign artists to paint them. There was an angry letter in the newspapers about that. Everybody thought you wrote it. The artists have been chosen to do the paintings. But you are not one of them."

"Mr. Morse, what is wrong?" Mr. Gale asked. "You are white as a sheet!"

"I'd like to be alone," Finley said.

For days he would see no one.

Not long after, there was more bad news. Someone in Europe was working on a telegraph, too! He and Gale must hurry. They wanted to be the first to make the telegraph famous.

"We *must* get a partner with money!" Mr. Gale said. "We need money to make many telegraphs, so people everywhere can use them."

Finley nodded. "First we must show a few important people what we can do with the telegraph. Then we'll get a rich partner, maybe three or four of them!"

They worked day and night getting ready. Inch by inch, they made three miles of wire. They rented a hall. They set up their telegraph machines. They invited a group of rich men to see the telegraph.

Finley made a short talk. "You gentlemen know that for hundreds of years men have signaled to each other. They have sent messages with smoke signals or flags or flashing lights. There is one trouble with all those kinds of signals."

"I know!" a man said. "On a foggy night, you can't signal as far as you can shout!"

"That's it!" Finley said. "My electromagnetic telegraph will change all that.

Why? Because *electricity will travel instantly through any known length of wire!* We have three miles of wire on that reel. I am going to send a message from this machine. The message will travel instantly through that wire. It will be written on the paper tape on that other machine. Professor Gale will read the message back to us."

"Of course!" a fat man said. "He knows the message!"

"Write one, yourself," Finley told him.

The man wrote. Finley sent the message. Mr. Gale picked up the tape on the other machine. He read the message.

The fat man stared. "Word for word! That's quite a stunt!"

Everybody smiled and clapped.

"Some day," Finley said, "we shall send messages that fast all over the United States!

All we need is the money to build the machines and lay the wires!"

When Finley said "money," the men stopped smiling. They got up. They thanked him for the "interesting stunt." They walked out.

The partners looked at each other. All that work for nothing! Now what?

The door opened. A young man came in. "Mr. Morse, I'm Alfred Vail. My family owns the Speedwell Iron Works in New Jersey. Would you like another partner? I could build you some better machines."

He started to say something more, but Finley and Mr. Gale were shaking his hands.

Alfred Vail built the machines. His father gave Finley and Alfred money to go to Washington. They showed the telegraph to the government.

Congressmen watched. The President and his cabinet watched. Everybody said it was an "interesting stunt." Nobody thought the government should spend any money on it.

Chapter *10*

Hard Times

Hard times struck the country. Banks closed. Businesses failed. Nobody had money to spend on the telegraph.

By 1842, Finley had worked ten years on his telegraph.

Once more, he and Mr. Gale tried to interest people. They made two miles of wire. They covered it with tar and rubber. One night, they laid it under water in New York harbor. It went from Battery Park to Governors Island.

The next morning, the newspapers told about it. At noon, messages would travel instantly through two miles of under-water cable. Everybody was invited to see the wonder of the ages!

Long before noon, the crowd gathered. Just before noon, something went wrong. Finley faced the excited people. He told them the telegraph had stopped working.

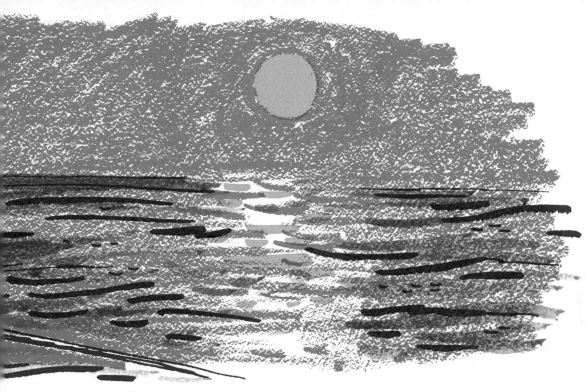

People jeered. They went away.

Later, the partners found what had happened. A ship's anchor had caught in the cable. The sailors did not know what it was. They cut it.

Finley had one last hope. Some congressmen were asking the government to spend $30,000 to test the telegraph. That would be enough money to lay a cable underground from Washington to Baltimore.

A congressman wrote to Finley. "I wish you could be here when Congress votes on the telegraph."

Finley hurried to Washington. He waited and waited. Congress had many other things to vote on. On March 3, Congress met for the last day.

A friend told Finley, "It's no use, Mr. Morse. They will not get around to voting on the telegraph this time."

Finley went back to the hotel. He counted his money. Tomorrow, he must pay his hotel bill. He must buy a ticket for New York. He would not have two dollars left.

The next morning, Annie Ellsworth, the daughter of a friend, came to see him. "Congratulations, Mr. Morse!"

"Why?"

"Congress voted 'yes' to the telegraph!

Some day, soon, you will send a message from Washington to Baltimore!"

"When I do," Finley promised, "you shall choose the message!"

Chapter *11*

Another Statue

A year later they were laying the underground line from Washington to Baltimore. They had the best wire, well-wrapped in cotton. They put it in lead pipe to protect it. Everything was perfect.

Then something went wrong. No electricity came through the line! They dug up some pipe. They cut it open. They found the trouble. At some time, the pipe had been too hot. The cotton on the wire was burned. The line was ruined.

What could they do? They had only $5,000 left. That was not enough to pay for another underground line. Could they put up poles, and stretch wires overhead? That would be cheaper. But would it be safe? They had to risk it.

On May 24, 1844, a crowd gathered in Washington. Finley sat before his telegraph machines. What if something went wrong? His hands shook.

Annie Ellsworth brought him a slip of paper. "Here is the message I want you to send, Mr. Morse."

He read it. He smiled. Somehow, it was a sign! His hands stopped shaking.

"Ladies and gentlemen," he said, "Miss Annie Ellsworth chose our message. She asked me to tell you what will happen.

"We have two machines here and two in Baltimore. This machine, with the paper tape, is the recorder. It writes the message.

"I send a message on this other machine. When I press down on it here, electricity flashes instantly to Baltimore. There, another recorder starts working. A pen marks the tape. If I press down just an instant, the pen in Baltimore makes a dot. If I press down a little longer, the pen in Baltimore makes a dash. The dots and dashes stand for letters.

"Now, I shall send the message. It will go forty miles to Baltimore. Then my partner will send it back to us."

Everybody leaned forward as Finley tapped out the message. Everybody sat back to wait.

Click! Click!

People jumped. They stared at the recorder. Only seconds had passed!

The tape stopped moving. Finley tore off the piece with dots and dashes marked on it. "There is the message I sent. 'WHAT HATH GOD WROUGHT!' "

Everybody stamped and cheered. At last, they believed in the telegraph!

Twenty-seven years later, there was a new statue in Central Park in New York. It was of Finley. The telegraphers of the United States and Canada had paid for it.

That June night in 1871, there was a big party. Finley sat there, trying to keep his mind on the speeches. "They call me 'eighty years young,' " he thought. "But after four speeches, I feel eighty years *old*!"

Every time a speaker said, "Samuel F. B. Morse!" the crowd clapped. Finley remembered his school days.

He sighed and felt the heavy medals on his chest. How many were there? He had lost count. He had been given medals from all over the world.

Medals . . . He thought of his first one. He remembered his statue of the Dying Hercules. He thought of the pictures he had stopped painting. But maybe it was better this way. All the world was linked with magic wires. Telegraph lines ran coast to coast. Under-water cables ran shore to shore. At last, three thousand miles of ocean could be passed over in an instant!

President Orton of the Western Union Company stood. "The time has come.

Every telegraph in the United States and Canada is waiting for this moment!"

A young lady came up to the machine on the stage. She sent Finley's greetings to telegraphers, everywhere.

Then Finley sat down at the telegraph. He tapped out, "S. F. B. Morse." He stood.

Everybody in the hall stood, too, cheering.

"Yes," Finley thought again, "perhaps this was better. Perhaps this was the way for me to 'be a credit.' "

But he thought again of his first medal.